T0038650

THE HOUSE
OF BEING

THE HOUSE
OF BEING

NATASHA TRETHEWEY

THE 2022 WINDHAM-CAMPBELL LECTURE

YALE UNIVERSITY PRESS
NEW HAVEN AND LONDON

The *Why I Write* series is published
with assistance from the Windham-
Campbell Literature Prizes, which
are administered by the Beinecke Rare
Book and Manuscript Library at
Yale University.

This volume is published with assistance
from the foundation established in memory of James Wesley Cooper of the Class
of 1865, Yale College.

Copyright © 2024 by Natasha Trethewey.
All rights reserved.

This book may not be reproduced, in
whole or in part, including illustrations,
in any form (beyond that copying permitted by Sections 107 and 108 of the U.S.
Copyright Law and except by reviewers
for the public press), without written
permission from the publishers.

Yale University Press books may be purchased in quantity for educational, business, or promotional use.
For information, please e-mail
sales.press@yale.edu (U.S. office) or
sales@yaleup.co.uk (U.K. office).

Printed in the United States of America.

ISBN 978-0-300-26592-7
(hardcover : alk. paper)
Library of Congress Control
Number: 2023944302

A catalogue record for this book is avail-
able from the British Library.

This paper meets the requirements
of ANSI/NISO Z39.48-1992
(Permanence of Paper).

10 9 8 7 6 5 4 3 2 1

Epigraph, and page 51: "Often I Am Permitted to Return to a Meadow," by Robert Duncan, from *The Opening of the Field*, copyright © 1960 by Robert Duncan; reprinted by permission of New Directions Publishing Corp.

pages 22, 67, 69: "Miscegenation," "Graveyard Blues," and "Monument," from *Native Guard*, by Natasha Trethewey, copyright © 2006 by Natasha Trethewey; reprinted by permission of HarperCollins Publishers.

page 35: Lucille Clifton, "study the masters," from *How to Carry Water: Selected Poems*, copyright © 2020 by The Estate of Lucille T. Clifton; reprinted with the permission of The Permissions Company, LLC, on behalf of BOA Editions, Ltd., boaeditions.org.

page 57: "Accounting," from *Memorial Drive: A Daughter's Memoir,* by Natasha Trethewey, copyright © 2020 Natasha Trethewey; reprinted by permission of HarperCollins Publishers.

page 60: Lisel Mueller, "When I Am Asked," from *Alive Together: New and Selected Poems,* Louisiana State University Press, 1996.

page 74: Natasha Trethewey, "Limen," from *Domestic Work,* copyright © 1998, 2000 by Natasha Trethewey; reprinted with the permission of The Permissions Company, LLC, on behalf of Graywolf Press, graywolf-press.org.

Often I am permitted to return to a meadow
as if it were a given property of the mind
that certain bounds hold against chaos,

that is a place of first permission,
everlasting omen of what is.

— Robert Duncan

CONTENTS

THE HOUSE
OF BEING

1

The World Book

The first collection of books I ever encountered filled the shelves of the tall bookcase at the back of my grandmother's house. It stood just inside the doorway to the den, at the end of a long hallway. From floor to ceiling was an assortment of novels and plays, history, philosophy, and mythology from my parents' university years; a set of classic children's stories in several volumes; etiquette books, a group of pamphlets from the fifties about the proper dress and comportment of young ladies; an abridged dictionary, and the twenty-volume *World Book* encyclopedia, 1966. Bought for the year I was born, the set was meant to be commemorative, marking the beginning of my journey toward knowledge.

My grandmother had purchased the set after nearly a year of saving the S&H Green Stamps she received with each purchase at the grocery store. There had been other gifts to choose from, I was told, including bronzed baby shoes or a set of creamy white dishes embellished with a border of pink roses and leaves, but my mother had insisted on the encyclopedia. Pristine and stiff-spined, the set occupied an entire shelf of the bookcase. As soon as I was able to reach the volumes, I'd pull one down to look at the photographs inside, the pages crisp and glossy.

That the story of the *World Book*'s provenance was passed down to me from the beginning made it even more prized. I was enthralled with the title, the idea that a set of books could contain even a single year of the world beyond our house. The thought of what awaited me there ignited a longing that followed me — even into sleep — as I listened to my father's voice reciting a bedtime story: the myth of Odysseus and his many trials that I was certain my father had found among the pages in the many books on those shelves.

Our nightly ritual of stories from classical mythology was only part of the means by which my father meant to reveal the world to me. To prepare me for it, and for the inevitable trials to come, he was determined that I have an early understanding of the metaphorical nature of language. During the day, the natural world served as our classroom. Most afternoons, we took long walks during which I'd pick wildflowers for my mother and he would recite poetry. All along the way, he'd point out the flora and fauna we encountered, the vivid imagery inscribed in so many of the names: red-winged blackbird with its bright slash of feathers; mockingbird mimicking another bird's song; the word *daisy*, which he repeated, again and again, altering it just so until I heard—in the syllables of that single word—two distinct ones, *day's eye*. He'd been holding the flower aloft, and suddenly I could see the way it mimicked the sun: each white petal a ray of light; the yellow disc at its center our day's bright eye.

On those afternoons, long before I could read, I heard Yeats's "Sailing to Byzantium," Robert Hayden's "Those Winter Sundays," Wordsworth's "Lines Composed a Few Miles Above Tintern Abbey," even the epic poem *Beowulf*—first in Old English, then in translation—all in the cadences of my father's resonant voice. And though I could not always grasp at first their meanings, I trembled with excitement at the sounds:

An aged man is but a paltry thing,
A tattered coat upon a stick, unless
Soul clap its hands and sing, and louder sing
For every tatter in its mortal dress. . . .

Occasionally, my father would pause to explain a word, an image, the metaphor therein. Most often it was something he could illustrate with the things around us: on the roadside — evidence of its difficult crossing — the cracked shell on an old turtle, its tattered, mortal dress.

I carry with me still a dream of that time — the earliest I can remember from my childhood: *I am standing in the hall outside the room I share with my parents, my crib beneath the window next to their bed. It is night and the house is so quiet it seems that I am alone, or that everyone else is sleeping. The long hallway before me is a cave, tunneling through the darkness: the bookcase — I can just make it out — at its opposite end. And there, standing in the doorway — blocking it — is a figure the shape of a man made entirely of the crushed oyster shells, white and sharp-edged, that formed the driveway beside our house.*

It's a familiar scene, archetypal in its imagery, which is why — I think — it has stayed with me. I must have been only three years old when I had the dream, and so the contents of all those books were as yet unavailable to me. What had the dream meant back then? It's a question I've been trying to answer ever since. Because the imagery of dreams is figurative, metaphorical as all language is, it's easy to apply meaning over the course of one's life to make sense of not only the past but also the present.

I can't recall whether I had the dream on a night just after my father recited the story of Odysseus, the Cyclops and the cave, but I can hear the echoes between them: how the hero of the story, on her quest, must get past the obstacle blocking her path to the world. When I think back on it now, I can see that all the stories my father told me, each with some form of the hero's journey, must have taken root in my psyche, establishing early on the pattern to which my own journey would conform. If the message I learned then from the experience of Odysseus was that it would take cleverness to outpace whatever obstacles stood before me, the meaning of the dream would deepen over the years as I came to see it as a metaphor rooted not only within the classical tradition of Greek mythology, but also in a vernacular tradition: the quest for knowledge – for literacy – in slave narratives that was equated with personhood, citizenship, the ability to escape.

That the obstacle in my dream was made of oyster shells, the indigenous materials of my native geography, is also telling. *Location*, wrote Eudora Welty, *is the crossroads of circumstance.* Even in the dream I knew the *World Book* was there, waiting for me. I needed only to get to it.

2

Crossroads

For a few years when I was very young, my parents and I lived with my maternal grandmother in her shotgun house on a small plot of land just outside the city limits of my hometown, Gulfport, Mississippi. It was the house where my mother had waited out the long months of her pregnancy, the first house I entered when I left the hospital the day after I was born. The land on which it stood had been in my family for over half a century, since the area of town once called Griswold Community had been a settlement of former slaves after the Civil War. A hundred years later, though it had changed a great deal, the area still maintained a measure of its rural character. I remember waking up to the sounds of a rooster crowing, someone's hogs — loosed and roaming — rooting in the dirt beneath the house. Sometimes I'd hear my grandmother outside, the trill of her laughter as she chatted in the yard with Uncle Mun — a man, deaf from birth, who spoke only in percussive syllables, choked and guttural. Down the street, a single skinny cow grazed in a tiny yard behind a chain-link fence. I could hear it lowing.

In the decades of the early twentieth century when my grandmother was growing up there with her six siblings, the land and the house on it had abutted a pasture. The pasture had been there during my mother's childhood too. She remembered calling across it to my great-uncle and aunt on the other side or treading a path through it to their house. In faded black and white photographs of the house from the early 1950s I can see a fringe of field, nearly out of the frame — as on the edge of consciousness — my imagination filling in the rest.

By the time I was born, the pasture was gone — paved over to make way for new Highway 49 — and the house now stood at a crossroads: the intersection of 49, a legendary highway of the Blues, and Jefferson Street.

There, in North Gulfport, on either side of the highway the streets that ran east and west were named for states; the north–south streets for presidents. On every corner, four-foot-tall concrete pillars, sunk deep in the ground and painted white, bore their names — like monuments to the founding of the nation, the complex ideals embedded therein. It was one of the myriad ways the landscape of my native geography was inscribed with one version of America while simultaneously subsuming or erasing others. The marker representing Thomas Jefferson was directly in front of my grandmother's property, at the edge of the shell driveway, a few steps from her mailbox — the fading letters of her name a faint impression, bleached in the sun.

If the marker gestured toward the idea of the classical, the monumental, my grandmother's house at the crossroads was the embodiment of a figurative, vernacular tradition. A double shotgun, the house was divided by a long hallway that ran the length of it, ending at the kitchen in the back: the living spaces on the left side, the work-related rooms on the right. Before my grandmother added on to it, the house had been a single shotgun characterized by rooms that are directly connected, without hallways—one room opening into the next. "Long, like the barrel of a shotgun," my father said. "You can fire straight through it, front to back."

The long hallway she'd added to the other half of the house had no windows. On one side of it, doors opened into the bedrooms; on the other side was an unbroken expanse of wall upon which my grandmother practiced her vernacular art. At the fabric store she bought bolts of cloth printed with natural scenes—views of distant mountains, close-up images of owls on snow-covered boughs—and attached them to sheets of plywood the size of large windows. She added oil paint to some areas to give texture; to make the scenes life-like, she affixed pinecones and branches with glue. The effect was a gallery of picture windows: scenes she might have dreamed of seeing outside her own. I understood it even then as a desire to make something beautiful of that hallway, to transform it, and I understood the act of imagination it took to look not simply *at* the pictures, but *through* them into a world we'd made that was different from the actual world we inhabited.

It's significant to me now that the house itself represented a vernacular tradition, as if it were something
I could internalize by osmosis. Though the origin of
the shotgun name is contested, scholars assert that the
long-house format is a legacy of West African architecture, brought to America by both free and enslaved peo-
ples who arrived in New Orleans from Haiti, after the
Revolution in 1804. That it was situated at the meeting place of Jefferson Street and Highway 49 is also
symbolic, indicative of the journey toward what would
become my abiding concerns. Big Joe Williams had
inscribed Highway 49 into the lexicon of the Blues with
his 1935 song of the same name. Emblematic in Blues
mythology, 49 was part of the crossroads where – in
an apocryphal story – the legendary guitarist Robert
Johnson was said to have sold his soul to the devil. The
problem with the myth, though quaint, is that it under-
mines not only the genuine aptitude and creativity that
Johnson possessed, but also his *studied* skill, a result of
practice and the mastery of his craft.

In more ways than one, in the shotgun house
at the intersection of Jefferson and 49, the folkways

and idioms of the African American vernacular tradition met the "received knowledge" of Enlightenment thinking and colonial culture, the language of Thomas Jefferson.

I'm gone get up in the morning / and hit the Highway 49, Big Joe Williams sang, *I've been looking for my woman / Lord, don't think she can be found.*

Among the blacks is misery enough, God knows, but no poetry, Jefferson wrote.

Geography, wrote Ralph Ellison, *is fate.*

Inevitably, individuals are shaped by the history and culture of inherited places. Applying Ellison's words to the happenstance of that intersection allows me to see my beginnings there as destiny. But I know it's a kind of magical thinking to look back and assign meaning to a constellation of circumstances: my birth on the hundredth anniversary of Confederate Memorial Day—in a place like Mississippi—the product of an interracial marriage; my early habitation in a house at the cross-roads. My need to make meaning from the geography of my past is not unlike the ancients looking to the sky at the assortment of stars and drawing connections between them: the constellations they named inscribing a network of stories that gave order and meaning to their lives. That's one of the reasons I write. I've needed to create the narrative of my life — its abiding metaphors — so that my story would not be determined for me.

There's a scene in Richard Wright's memoir *Black Boy* in which he is answering a question posed to him by a white woman from whom he is seeking employment: "Well, I want to be a writer," he says. "You'll never be a writer," she says. "Who on earth put such ideas into your nigger head?" Though the scene initially spoke to me as evidence of our shared experience as black Mississippians, decades apart — the book was published the year my mother was born — it would come back to me, years later, for a different reason. But at first, I saw only a reflection of my own time and place: a Deep South still mired in myth and steeped in metaphors rooted in a matrix of selective memory, willed amnesia, and racial determinism.

A year before I was born, at the centennial of the Civil War, major civil rights legislation had been enacted – the Civil Rights and Voting Rights Acts of 1964 and '65 – advancing the march toward freedom for black Americans. It was a violent crossroads in Mississippi, a critical moment in which the laws were changing, but the iconic symbol of white supremacy and black oppression, the Confederate flag, would still be enlisted to send an emphatic message, emblematic of a place determined to maintain a collective narrative about its people and history. In the century following the war, the habits of mind rooted in white suprem-acy – its metaphors – had become even more deeply entrenched.

Robert Penn Warren, writing at the centennial, described the metaphors white Southerners had come to live by as "the Great Alibi," locating the Confederacy's defeat as the moment "the Solid South was born," a "City of the Soul" rendered guiltless – in the white mind of the South – by the forces of history. "The South," he wrote, "explains, condones, and transmutes every-thing . . ." "Even now, any common lyncher becomes a defender of the Southern tradition . . . bloodlust rising from a matrix of boredom and resentful misery becomes a high sense of honor, and ignorance becomes divine revelation. . . . defeat turns into victory, defects into virtues. . . . And the most painful and costly consequences of the Great Alibi are found, of course, in connection with race."

Because the "Solid South" was a society based on the myths of innate racial difference, a hierarchy based on notions of supremacy, the language used to articulate that thinking was rooted in the unique experience of white southerners. The role of metaphor is not only to describe the experience of reality; metaphor also shapes how we perceive reality. Thus, in the decades following the war, the South – in the white mind of the South – was deeply entrenched in the idea of a noble and romantic past. It was moonlight and magnolias, chivalry and paternalism. The blacks living within her borders, when they were good, were "children" to be guided, looked after, protected from their own folly, "mules" of the earth, "darkies" with the "light of service" in their hearts. When they stepped out of line they were "bad niggers" from whom white women – carriers of the pure bloodline – needed to be protected; they were "animals" to be husbanded into a prison system modeled on the plantation system. On the monumental landscape they were unstoried but for the stories told about them: misapprehensions that rendered them, in the mind of the South, "passive recipients of white benevolence" who "never fought for their own freedom" – even as nearly 200,000 fought for the Union in the Civil War. And when they were exceptional in the mind of the South, they were magical: *You're pretty for a black girl, smart for a black girl, not like the rest of them.*

George Orwell wrote, "Who controls the past controls the future. Who controls the present controls the past." In positioning themselves as "guardians of the past," an organization of Southern white women, the United Daughters of the Confederacy, was instrumental in the creation of the abiding metaphors of the white mind of the South, the "hallowed falsehoods" – as the historian John Hope Franklin put it – that served as the white South's intellectual justification for its ongoing subjugation of black Americans. In the last two decades of the nineteenth century and the first two of the twentieth, they set out to inscribe a dominant narrative on the landscape and in the minds of schoolchildren – indeed into the American imagination. Through the erecting of monuments, and the naming of roads, bridges, and other public works, they constructed a physical and psychic landscape that promoted white supremacy, memorialized the myth of a virtuous Confederate cause, and wrote black Americans out of the story—despite black soldiers' role in the Civil War, in preserving the Union. The history textbooks commissioned by the UDC—ones I'd later read in school—glorified the institution of slavery and devoted little time to Reconstruction and the horrors inflicted upon black Americans throughout the Jim Crow era.

No aspect of public life was beyond the organization's reach. The state flag of Mississippi, incorporating the Confederate battle flag in its canton, was a daily visual reminder of white Mississippians' allegiance to the state's slaveholding heritage and the war fought and lost to maintain it—its message a kind of synecdoche, the small part in the upper corner standing in for the whole: that Mississippi would not be inclusive of all its citizens except in the ongoing narrative of white dominion over black subjects. And it was a symbol indicative of the new ways the state would find to maintain the second-class status of black Americans.

———

When I arrived at the house at the crossroads, the day after the hundredth anniversary of Confederate Memorial Day, the flags flown to celebrate the holiday glorifying the mythology of a "virtuous" *Lost Cause* punctuated the landscape – alongside the state flag of Mississippi – waving an implicit message: *Know your place.* Despite the passage of the Civil Rights Act, my parents' interracial marriage was still illegal in Mississippi and in as many as twenty other states in the nation, rendering me illegitimate in the eyes of the law – *persona non grata*. As in W. H. Auden's memorial to William Butler Yeats – *Mad Ireland hurt you into poetry* – Mississippi inflicted my first wound.

When I contemplate my earliest years in that time and place, I am reminded of Orwell's notion of the importance of the historical moment in which a writer lives: that "revolutionary, tumultuous times" will have a profound impact on subject matter, and that before a writer even begins to write "[s]he will have acquired an emotional attitude from which [s]he will never completely escape." Though I can remember the evening that I lay between my parents, examining their color differences, I know that it could not have been the first moment of recognition, that some awareness of the world must have been building in me, an accumulation of experience that led me to ask them: *What am I?* Holding their hands up, side by side, it was as though I were weighing them on some immovable scale by which — I had by then begun to see — they had already been measured. (My question might as well have meant: *how am I to be measured?*)

Children enter the sensemaking world through language, by naming things. Early on, my father had taught me that there is a word in the language for everything, and my question — *What am I?* — demanded a word.

The word for the crossroads that was my parents' marriage, *miscegenation,* entered the American lexicon during the Civil War in a pamphlet. It had been conceived as a hoax by a couple of journalists to drum up opposition to the re-election of Abraham Lincoln through the threat of amalgamation and mongrelization. A century later, though unwritten, the word haunted the margins of the vital record of my birth — the afterimage of the document's official language, its measured syntax. Perhaps because miscegenation was illegal and the former governor Ross Barnett was still monitoring interracial activity in the state, the clerk who filled out the birth certificate recorded the race of my mother as *Colored,* and my white father, *Canadian.*

One would have only to look at the language to begin to unravel the history and the attendant mythology at once concealed and revealed within a single word. Ezra Pound coined the phrase *luminous details* to describe such transcendentals in an array of facts — those things capable of providing "a sudden insight into circumjacent conditions, into their causes, their effects, into sequence, and law." On my birth certificate, a designation of nationality was meant to conceal the race of my father; a luminous detail among an array of ordinary vital facts, it revealed much more about the world, the time and place I had entered.

A birth certificate is the first page of a life story, an origin myth. I don't know when I first read the language of mine nor do I recall my initial encounter with the word *miscegenation,* but I can trace backward my interest in the etymology of words, the myths and metaphors embedded in our language — as well as the absences, omissions, and erasures of history — to that

THE AUTHOR WITH HER PARENTS,
ERIC TRETHEWEY AND GWENDOLYN TRETHEWEY,
OUTSIDE HER GRANDMOTHER'S HOUSE IN 1966

first written page on which my name appears. My poem "Miscegenation" is an answer to that first page, the unwritten implications of it: a rewriting of the "official" narrative.

MISCEGENATION

In 1965 my parents broke two laws of Mississippi;
they went to Ohio to marry, returned to Mississippi.

They crossed the river into Cincinnati, a city whose name
begins with a sound like *sin*, the sound of wrong — *mis* in Mississippi.

A year later they moved to Canada, followed a route the same
as slaves, the train slicing the white glaze of winter, leaving Mississippi.

Faulkner's Joe Christmas was born in winter, like Jesus, given his name
for the day he was left at the orphanage, his race unknown in Mississippi.

My father was reading *War and Peace* when he gave me my name.
I was born near Easter, 1966, in Mississippi.

When I turned 33 my father said, *It's your Jesus year — you're the same
age he was when he died.* It was spring, the hills green in Mississippi.

I know more than Joe Christmas did. Natasha is a Russian name —
though I'm not; it means *Christmas child*, even in Mississippi.

The language of the poem transforms the notion of the illegal — thus *illegitimate* — birth into a sacred one, like the birth of Christ. The comparison is manifest in the repetition of the rhymed words *name* and *same* in each of the stanzas following the establishment of the refrain word, *Mississippi*, in the first couplet: name/same/name/name/same/name. The poem examines place, history, law, the Gospel. It is both a literary autobiography and creation myth rooted in books: Faulkner's *Light in August*, Tolstoy's *War and Peace*, the Bible. Gesturing toward a vernacular tradition, the poem echoes the freedom journey often recounted in slave narratives: crossing the Ohio River into the North, even on to Canada — as well as the journey toward literacy. The many threads of an origin story are pulled together by the form — a *ghazal* — the elegant envelope that makes articulation possible: a necessary utterance, the disparate parts shaped into meaning.

———

If my father meant to instill in me a way—through a thorough grasp of the metaphorical nature of language—to contend with the cultural onslaught of my native land, my mother had for me a different kind of lesson. She knew well the various means that white Mississippians employed, both legally and extralegally, to maintain black subordination and White Supremacy. She'd grown up in the era of Jim Crow segregation and had been eleven years old in 1955 when Emmett Till was murdered. A photograph taken outside the courthouse in Sumner, where the trial of the men accused of Till's abduction and murder was held, shows a large gathering of African Americans. They stand at the entrance to the courthouse or sit at the base of the Confederate monument on the lawn. You can see the words "Our Heroes" emblazoned beneath the battle flag graven there. Though you cannot see the state flag, it hangs there too. Together, the flags presided over the message soon to be delivered: the all-white jury's acquittal of Roy Bryant and J. W. Milam, the men who would later brag to *Look* magazine about murdering the child. There is yet another message, implicit in the imagery of the photograph. If the Confederate battle flag alone could signify virulent and dangerous forms of White

Supremacy, as it has increasingly over the years, the communion of the state flag of Mississippi and the battle flag was no less meaningful, but insidious in its signifying.

It was the ongoing onslaught of implicit messages—that the lives of black people mattered less than the lives of whites—that my mother was intent on countering as we navigated a landscape rife with it. Whenever we passed the state flag, often driving down the beach road that had been dedicated, on a plaque erected by the Daughters of the Confederacy, as "The Jefferson Davis Memorial Highway," my mother would sing to me the "Battle Hymn of the Republic"—the anti-slavery, abolitionist version that morphed into an anthem for Union troops during the Civil War: *John Brown's body lies a-mouldering in the grave, / . . . but his truth is marching on.* Although in some versions it's Brown's *soul* that is marching on, she sang the lyrics that implied an *ongoing* struggle for justice:

> Oh, soldiers of freedom, then strike while strike you may
> The deathblow of oppression in a better time and way;
> For the dawn of old John Brown was brightened into day,
> And his truth is marching on.

She had learned the song, along with "Lift Every Voice and Sing," the black national anthem, in a segregated school. During the Jim Crow era of her childhood, the teaching of these songs in black schools was part of a counter-education — what the scholar Jarvis Givens termed a "fugitive pedagogy." Singing to me as we passed the state flag of Mississippi was a way to counteract the symbolic, psychic violence of it. Through the triumphant, stirring rhythms of the song, my mother was showing me how to signify, how to use received forms to challenge the dominant cultural narrative of our native geography, and to transcend it by imagining a reality in which justice was possible. Her voice was a counterweight.

Homo sapiens, wrote E. O. Wilson, *is the only species to suffer psychological exile.* Perhaps that is the existential condition of all poets. The act of writing is a way to create another world in language, a dwelling place for the psyche wherein the chaos of the external world is transformed, shaped into a *made* thing, and ordered. It is an act of reclamation. And resistance: the soul sings for justice and the song is poetry.

3

The House of Being

Beside my desk, I keep several artifacts: photographs of my parents with me in the yard at the house on Jefferson Street, a set of hot combs, and a calendar from my grandmother's first business, Lee's Beauty Salon.

When my mother was a girl, the front room of the house was the beauty parlor. The calendar features a picture of her, six years old, her name beneath it. But for the rusted staples holding the tear-off months in place, the calendar is pristine — preserved in a frame against acid-free paper, behind museum glass. No pages have been torn from it, stopping time at January 1952. On my wall, it's a type of memorial, the frame I've placed it

Gwendolyn Ann Turnbough

LEE'S BEAUTY SALON

Mrs. Loretta Turnbough, Prop.

PHONE 2539-J

110 EAST JEFFERSON STREET   GULFPORT, MISSISSIPPI

JANUARY · 1952

in a monument—not only to my mother, but also to the place it represents. I can see now that this has always been one of my impulses: to remember, to make a container for the vanished past—the forgotten or erased. I could not have known that in the beginning, but the circumstances all around me were leading me there.

By the time I arrived at the house, my grandmother was a drapery seamstress. She had long closed the doors of the beauty parlor and taken a job downtown at a drapery factory. The day I was born, she quit the factory job and opened her own drapery business so that she could look after me. Her large workroom now occupied the front of the house, every inch of it filled with notions: jars of buttons; bolts of ribbon, fringe, and trim; spools of thread, arranged by color and shade, in shadow boxes along the walls; needles and bobbins, pins and hooks and eyes. In the center of the room there was a great cutting table and three Singer sewing machines; along the perimeter, a chifforobe and cedar chests where she kept patterns for dressmaking. The space beneath the table was stacked with bolts of cloth, remnants in every color, texture, and pattern—her vast stores of material. Above it, the pristine surface on which she worked white as a blank page.

I spent countless hours in that workroom, watching my grandmother at her machines or the cutting table while my parents were at work. She designed all kinds of window treatments — cornices and swags and shades — and I loved the different words for them, as well as the words for various fabrics, stitches, pleat folds, and decorative notions. She'd hum while holding pins in her mouth, her foot working the pedal of the sewing machine, a rhythm in counterpoint. If I was in the next room, my playroom, I'd listen to the sound the machine made, knowing exactly when she was sewing a long straight line — how it sped up or slowed down, depending on the difficulty of joining several layers of fabric, or when she turned a corner before beginning another long line of stitches.

In my playroom there was a large toybox with two rows of shelves above it. With fabric and cardboard and trim, I'd create little interiors on one of the shelves, decorating each room — as my grandmother did — and making up stories about the lives of the people who would inhabit them. The other shelf housed the books I'd make — each one held together with ribbon, the pages yet empty but for my name on the frontispiece. I held them in a kind of reverence: monumental

THE AUTHOR'S GRANDMOTHER, LERETTA

objects waiting for what I would inscribe there. Why does it sting me now, that — in the years to come — they remained that way, that I never returned to them, never wrote in them a thing?

Watching my grandmother's craftsmanship, I was learning something about the necessity for precision: how to look for loose or uneven stitches, the just articulation as the designs on patterned fabric, when pieced together, matched seamlessly to the eye. To create that seamless blending of form, she made precise measures and cuts so that no material was wasted, nothing was out of place: the patterns true, the result a thing of beauty. That translates to me now as a way to think about syntax, about order and chaos: *how* one writes is inseparable from *why* one does.

All those lessons, inadvertently learned in my grandmother's workroom, would come back to me when I began to write: my foot tapping the floor to the rhythm of syntax the way hers tapped the pedal of the Singer; what I knew of her life guiding me toward my first collection of poems, *Domestic Work*. Her earliest job had been as a domestic: she and her sisters taking in wash; trapping, gutting, and delivering crabs to the back doors of white people's homes; cooking and cleaning.

Over her lifetime, each new job she held — from elevator operator to beautician, to drapery seamstress in a factory and, finally, self-employment — represented her tireless striving. She'd grown up during the Depression, which is perhaps why she seemed always to define herself by the work of her hands. Her stories were filled with the details of the labor she and her siblings had done, not merely for survival in the Jim Crow South, but because of an abiding belief in the nobility of it. They were among the great numbers of the African American working class whose labors helped to build the nation and keep it running. *The story of the Negro in America,* wrote James Baldwin, *is the story of America.*

When I think of my grandmother at her work, I am reminded of a poem by Lucille Clifton:

study the masters

like my aunt timmie.
it was her iron,
or one like hers,
that smoothed the sheets
the master poet slept on.
home or hotel, what matters is
he lay himself down on her handiwork

and dreamed.   she dreamed too,   words:
some cherokee, some masai and some
huge and particular as hope.
if you had heard her
chanting as she ironed
you would understand form and line
and discipline and order and
america.

In the poem's intersection of the "handiwork" of
Aunt Timmie, her languages, and the implied work
of the master poet, I find an echo of the crossroads
of knowledge I encountered in the house on Jefferson
Street. There, I was learning more than one way of
knowing and more than one language: what my father,
a poet, would have called the "King's English," and the
black vernacular—intimate, familial—that my mother
and grandmother spoke only at home, to each other
or to neighbors who stopped by to visit after church.
I could hear the different way my grandmother spoke
with her customers when they came to her workroom,
and the way my mother spoke when we shopped downtown. Even then I was beginning to see, in ways that my
father could not, the value of both: the way that stan-

THE AUTHOR'S GRANDMOTHER ON THE
SEGREGATED BEACH IN GULFPORT, MISSISSIPPI

dard English carries a currency (that can disadvantage non-speakers), but also the way black English connects one to family and community and place with its unique cadences and rhythms of syntax, timing and rhetorical style, idioms and metaphors—the province of the poet. Each is rooted in a particular history, with—as James Baldwin put it—different realities to "articulate, or control."

Listening to my grandmother and acquiring both languages, I was learning the power in the ability to codeswitch; but I was learning a hierarchy too. Though my father wanted to rid me fully of black English, I resisted; as a child I knew only that, because I loved the people who spoke it, I was not willing to give up the language that connected us across time and space. I was not willing to give up what I had learned *studying* my grandmother.

———

In the years to come, the days spent at my grandmother's house were a constant in my life, even after my parents' divorce. Though my mother and I had moved to Atlanta so that she could begin graduate school, I spent every summer back home in Mississippi, just to be with my grandmother and to visit my father in New Orleans. When my mother remarried, my grandmother's house became a refuge, the three months of summer a respite. For the nine months of the school year, I lived in a household where I was a kind of outsider, isolated by my stepfather Joel, a troubled Vietnam veteran who was jealous of my mother's previous marriage and contemptuous of me. There were great silences in that house, and a dark undercurrent of domestic violence — I would come to discover — from which my mother was determined to protect me.

At my grandmother's house I could relax, and I'd spend a good deal of my time in solitary reverie, as the dreamy child does, exercising what my father would call "my inner resources." I could sit down to read and lose myself — all without fear of the chronic tensions I'd left behind in Atlanta. An introduction to the world of knowledge lay open before me in the pages of a book.

When I arrive at the memory of that time, I am led back to the summer I was nine years old, determined to read as many entries in the *World Book* as I could — a way I thought to be worldly, to escape my own circumstances and imagine myself instead on the steps of the Parthenon, touring the ruins of history, or in Parliament, debating the important issues of the time.

What led me to the entry for "Races of Man"? Perhaps I had been looking for it. Until then, my knowledge about the perceptions of race, racial difference and hierarchy, was still anecdotal, not academic, gleaned mostly from my experience growing up in the Deep South in the late sixties and seventies: the way white people in Mississippi had often stared at me and my parents with disgust or contempt; the way my grandmother had not been permitted to try on hats at the department store as white women were; the words I'd heard loud on the playground at school or whispered at the movie theater, dime store, Piggly Wiggly: *mongrel, half-breed, nigger lover.* Words that said to me: *you are an aberration and your white father—loving your black mother—is degraded, worthy of a slur.*

What did I hope to find in the *World Book*?

At the top of the page, I read the words, "Basic types: Caucasoid, Mongoloid, Negroid," followed by descriptions of hair texture, eye shape, color; what were supposed to be distinguishing racial characteristics—that if you were white, the ratio of femur to tibia was different than if you were black. In one race (the authors asserted) the femur is longer, in the other the tibia. In the illustrations, the Caucasoid type was represented by what seemed to be the head of a classical Roman statue; even in black and white, he seemed carved from Parian marble, his head tilted as in contemplation. The others were rendered primitives, the image of the Negro almost photographic; a specimen, he seemed to look straight ahead as in the pictures I'd later see of enslaved people, their innermost thoughts held in secret behind a blank stare. Even more than the text, it's the collection of images that has stayed with me, a taxonomy. Starting where the entry began, white was first, at the top; black was last, at the bottom. When the images varied from this hierarchy, white was centered as though it were the standard against which the others were measured. The interplay between image and word — *Caucasoid, Mongoloid, Negroid* — was telling me everything about the world I inhabited. I knew something was wrong, but I had not yet fully rejected it, had not yet begun to resist the calcified manifestations of received knowledge even as I was already on a journey toward self-knowledge: knowledge based not only in experience, but also in the cultivation of the intellect.

In that moment, armed with the encyclopedia's combination of traits — the purported rubric for determining what I was, my place within the racial hierarchy represented in the visual language — I sneaked into my grandmother's workroom, found her tape measure, and held it against my leg.

If encountering the daily onslaught of white supremacy in the symbolic language inscribed on the landscape of my native geography was a kind of psychic violation, so then was finding evidence of those ideas in the encyclopedia's pages. Before that, as a small child, I had only believed in what I imagined to be the sanctity of books — repositories of knowledge, a higher plane of thought — wherein, across time and space, the greatest and most enduring ideas had been recorded. Because I'd not yet fully grasped what my father was intent on teaching me — the figurative nature of language, my own habitation in it — I did not yet have a means by which to push back against what I read in the *World Book* and to articulate a notion of self not proscribed by language meant to define me. Therein lay the danger Robert Frost articulated in his essay "Education by Poetry."

"What I am pointing out," Frost wrote, "is that unless you are at home in the metaphor, unless you have had your proper poetical education in the metaphor, you are not safe anywhere. Because you are not at ease with figurative values: you don't know the metaphor in its strength and its weakness. You don't know how far you may expect to ride it and when it may break down with you. You are not safe in science; you are not safe in history."

By *science*, Frost is referring, in the largest sense, to *knowledge* — philosophy, the science of thought. Part of my habitation in language began with the metaphors of the mind of the white South — the received knowledge of the region, seemingly discreet, informed by the inhabitants' perceptions of their lived experience, and yet not: it is also a "knowledge" whose roots stretch back centuries and across space as well as time. Through the knowledge production of Enlightenment scientists such as Linnaeus and philosophers such as Kant and Hume, one can chart the codification of racial difference and hierarchy, the roots of nineteenth-century scientific racism, and the bedrock of ongoing, deeply ingrained, and often unexamined contemporary notions of racial difference — received knowledge become synonymous with truth.

What the *World Book* taught me was only one of many lessons that set me on a path toward becoming a writer. How many times, over the years, would my father remind me — quoting Martin Heidegger — that "Language is the house of being"? It would be decades before I'd read those words myself in a book by the German philosopher — who was *also* a member of the Nazi Party — and feel again that sharp pang of recognition: the difficult knowledge that some of the most enduring ideas had been written by complicated figures, like Thomas Jefferson, who believed in racial hierarchies, inherent superiority and inferiority. More and more I would come to understand that it was not simply ignorance that I'd need to push back against, but also the stores of received knowledge — philosophy, history, science — that I would encounter in the most learned places.

4

Native Pastures

Despite the highway running right beside our plot of land, my grandmother's house seemed nestled in a small wood of mimosa, persimmon, and pecan trees. Bordered by a ditch that often overflowed after rain, the house sat two feet off the ground, perched on cinder blocks — seemingly unattached from the land — its tenuous footing just above the inevitable threat of water in a landscape frequented by hurricanes. I remember one morning opening the back door off the kitchen after a storm and seeing nothing but water where the backyard had been. The water had come up to the threshold and the house seemed to float there, on the verge of being swept away, out into the Gulf of Mexico. Standing in the doorway I found my own reflection in place of the steps, and, for a moment, I could imagine everything — our whole community — gone. It was the first inkling I had of being grounded in a particular place, tethered to it despite the absence of a visible, solid foundation. Looking across the field of water was perhaps the first moment I began to register, consciously, the nature of impermanence that would later translate into my need to inscribe our presence on the landscape, to hold on to what might otherwise be lost, what was already disappearing.

It was 1969: the year a hurricane hit, the year I had begun to ask questions about race, the year of the dream in which a figure made of crushed oyster shells blocked my path to the bookshelves — the *World Book* — at the back of the house. A photograph from that time shows me with my parents in the living room of my grand-mother's house. I've written about it many times, each time encountering something new that it reveals to me about the past, our lives, the historical moment in which it was taken. I am interested in the rift between what the subjects of the photograph knew in the moment of its making and all the things to come that they could not know, the heartbreak of that. A photograph is a kind of elegy, framing and memorializing what is gone, capturing a fleeting moment. In the moment our photograph was taken, I did not know that my parents were only a few years from divorce. What I remember most about that day was the photographer, a double amputee. He exists outside the frame, on the other side of the lens, but the memory of him there shaped the first poem I wrote about the photograph as much as what I'd come to know later. It represents the intersection between what is there and not there, like the phantom limb ache of something gone but still palpably present.

FAMILY PORTRAIT

Before the picture man comes
Mama and I spend the morning
cleaning the family room. She hums
Motown, doles out chores, a warning—

He has no legs, she says. *Don't stare.*
I'm first to the door when he rings.
My father and uncle lift his chair
onto the porch, arrange his things

near the place his feet would be.

He poses our only portrait — my father

sitting, Mama beside him, and me

in between. I watch him bother

the space for knees, shins, scratching air

as — years later — I'd itch for what's not there.

When I wrote "Family Portrait," one of my earliest poems, I was thinking only about the dissolution of my family, my parents' union, something that I had seemingly been able to adjust to such that I could liken it to an itch — an uneasy, restless desire for what was gone, akin to a vexing longing. In considering the relationship of title to text, a reader — knowing nothing of my personal history — would be able to glean the metaphor of loss as dissolution of the family. Beneath the photographer's gesture, however, was something darker, more painful: the loss of a once-living part of himself. I'd not consciously allowed my mother's death to enter the poem, but of course it was there.

When I returned to the photograph in a later book of poems, I was concerned with the gestures of my parents, the lordly way my father is positioned, his hand

THE AUTHOR WITH HER PARENTS IN THE LIVING ROOM
OF HER GRANDMOTHER'S HOUSE IN 1969

draped easily over me; my mother balanced on the small arm of the chair, pressing her finger into my arm as if not only to still me but also to leave an indelible imprint. The juxtaposition of his large white hand, her small brown finger. The photograph suggested to me the ways that — in the public narrative of who I was as a poet — my mother, dead for so long, was being erased yet again, as if her imprint on me was smaller than that of my father. In articles written *about* me, it was as though I'd become a poet simply because my father was a poet, that the ability to write had been handed down through him and not in any way influenced by my mother's impact on me: the gendered and racial implications of that. It was not unlike all the things I had heard white people say when I was growing up whenever I did anything well: *Oh, that's your white side* or *You're not like the rest of them.* To which I'd say: *Who do you mean by the rest of them? My mother? My grandmother?*

Looking at the photograph now, I am struck by my own impish gesture — how playful and comfortable I seem, between them. *Every feeling waits upon its gesture,* wrote Eudora Welty.

Over the years, I've lost most photographs to the devastations of hurricanes, fire, my mother's death:

disasters both natural and manmade. When I sift through the images of my past, I realize that the only photographs I have of me with my parents are taken at the house at the crossroads, as if the location itself was the only true space for *our* being that could contain it. Even though I have recollections of us in other places, the evidence that remains places us there. We are only together in the space that is for me both real and imagined. I am reminded of these lines from a poem by Robert Duncan:

> Often I am permitted to return to a meadow
> as if it were a given property of the mind
> that certain bounds hold against chaos,
>
> that is a place of first permission,
> everlasting omen of what is.

―――

When Henry James wrote to Edith Wharton, "Be tethered to native pastures, even if it reduces you to a backyard in New York," he was reminding her of the need to write from the places we come from, the places that have shaped us, our character, the folkways and idioms we inherit, our economic situation and our disposition toward it. I believe that he was also suggesting the need to remain tethered to the place of one's spiritual nourishment: not just the physical places from which we come, but that which is derived from the mind, a field of thought, the constitution of the intellect and the power of the imagination. The first time I undertook this exercise to examine why I write — a decade and a half ago — I don't think I understood that part. It's taken trying to address again this question I've answered many times in my writing life to see it now.

Somewhere in my personal archive is a series of drafts of a poem titled "Permanence." I began trying to write it when I was working on poems that would later compose my first book. This was before I had come to fully understand or acknowledge my own obsessions, the intersection of my existential wounds. There's a way, early on, that one can be driven as a writer to make certain choices about subject matter without fully understanding the scope and contours of that impulse. It has something to do with the patterns of thought and feeling that have been forming all along.

The poem focused on the fact of the positioning of my grandmother's house, its tenuous footing. Over several drafts, I was posing questions to myself about what would remain, after we were gone, to show that we had been here: *What will keep us from being erased, forgotten?* There was nothing in the drafts about the inscriptive, monumental landscape of the South in which I had been raised, its absences and violence both physical and psychic. Instead, the natural world was an ever-present symbol of erasure and impermanence – the way that water could overtake us, or the way that trees and shrubs and vines would overgrow the land where a house had stood before being destroyed and washed away in a storm. I was only three years old when Hurricane Camille devasted the Mississippi Gulf Coast, and I have vague memories of the powerful storm, of being carried from room to room as rain poured in through the roof: wind howling, the house shuddering as if it would collapse, the cacophony of water hitting the tin pans on the floor of every room. By morning, the house still stood, nearly intact, though across the street the roof had been torn from the church.

Perhaps that's one reason it was easier for me at first to focus, in that unfinished poem, on natural disasters, on nature as a *neutral* force. Easier not to acknowledge what else was lurking in my subconscious. In that way, I could interpret my early dream, the figure made of shells from our driveway, as only a manifestation of what could be wrought by the natural world. And yet, on that small plot of land, I know that I had become aware of the possibility of both natural and manmade disasters through the stories passed down to me by my family. Not only did I know from my grandmother of the former *presence* of the pasture abutting her land, I knew also of its *erasure* — that Highway 49 had replaced it, cutting through the heart of North Gulfport, and dividing the once close-knit community of her recollection. When I think of the trees hugging the backyard where I played, I find first an image of comfort, protection, but when I expand my view to take in the driveway beside the house, I see looming above it a giant billboard advertising *Marine Life* — half of its pilings sunk deep into the ground bordering our small plot of land, monument to the commercial world imminently encroaching. I recall, too, another family story: the night the Ku Klux Klan burned a cross there.

It would have been easy for someone driving by on Highway 49 to think the driveway was church property. It faced Mount Olive Baptist, directly across Jefferson Street, and on Sundays during worship hours my grandmother let the deacons park the church bus there.

For a few weeks one summer, while my parents and I were still living with her, the church elders had been holding a voter registration drive, signing up black citizens in the community. For this reason, we never knew if the act of domestic terrorism was directed at us, the interracial family in the house, or at the church for conducting the drive.

I was too young to remember the events of that night, but I grew up hearing the story. The cross burned until the flames died, and whatever ashes remained would have washed away or dissolved with time, the tufts of grass between the oyster shells springing up green again each season. Nature's way of erasing evidence of what happened, neutral—unlike the erasures wrought by humans with varying motives. Only our memory, our retelling the story year after year, served to keep an awareness of this troubling history alive.

The competing images of the landscape exist in my imagination like transparencies for an overhead projector: I place them one atop the other to change the backdrop of the house from pasture to highway, flaming cross to *Marine Life* sign—each layer a palimpsest.

What will keep us from being erased, forgotten?

When I first wrote those words, in a draft of "Permanence," I had not yet allowed myself to consciously acknowledge the deeper implications of the question. Still, though I hadn't yet begun to write about the manmade erasures everywhere around me, my impulse to make a lasting record, to inscribe on the landscape of American cultural and historical memory something of *us* – my family, my community – was in direct relationship to them. It would take me much longer to recognize what else was embedded in my question, which is why – I think – I could never finish the poem. I have found that an inability to confront some emotional truth in a poem is the thing that dooms it. "We make of the quarrel with others, rhetoric," wrote William Butler Yeats, "but of the quarrel with ourselves, poetry."

Even though I have come to locate the *need* to write in the moment of loss, my mother's death, there's a scene in my memoir, *Memorial Drive,* in which my early *desire* to write is placed in juxtaposition to her life:

ACCOUNTING

One day I come home from school giddy with news. It is early evening and the four of us take our seats at the kitchen table. Most days during the week I have practice after school and get home too late for these "family" dinners. Joel will already have left the house on those nights, so there are blessed stretches of days when I don't see him at all.

Tonight, though, I'm too excited to save my news for when I can tell my mother alone, so I blurt it out as soon as we sit down. Not only have I been promoted to editor on the newspaper staff, but also, because of a short story I wrote, I've been invited to join Quill and Scroll, the club responsible for putting out the high school literary journal. I can see the delight in my mother's face. She is smiling at me and I am like a daffodil, lifting my face to the sun. I go on about how much I love the short story reader we are using in English class, how John Updike's "A&P" is my favorite so far, how I am planning to write a new story for an upcoming issue. "I'm going to be a writer!" I announce.

"You not gonna do any of that," my stepfather says, shrugging his shoulders. He doesn't even look up from his plate when he says it. My mother is seated to my right and I see her out of the corner of my eye, a deep furrow between her brows, her jaw clenched so tight she seems to speak with her mouth closed: "She. Will do. WHATEVER. She wants."

I am stunned, my head bent now toward my own plate, afraid to look at her or provoke him further by meeting his eyes across the table. For years she has held her tongue, encouraging me mostly in private so as to avoid his jealous anger. This moment is different, and I know the cost. She's going to be beaten tonight for that, I think to myself, the tone — even inside my head — resigned, matter-of-fact.

The rest of dinner we eat in silence, Joel glowering, my mother in quiet defiance. I am stealing glances at her face, thinking of the bruises she'll wear tomorrow, all the hidden places on her body soft with pain, calculating the price she'll keep paying to save me.

I've replayed this scene in my head countless times: *She. Will do. WHATEVER. She wants.* Even now I hear in my mother's voice, her measured restraint, the origins of my own.

When I think of that scene, I am reminded again of the moment in *Black Boy* when Richard Wright declares he wants to be a writer, and what it means to have someone with a kind of dominion over you try to diminish you by telling you what you cannot do or be. It must have been around the same time that I read the book. Wright's hunger for the free and unfettered expression of the self—in the midst of trauma both personal and national—spoke to me deeply of my own experience.

In only a few more years my mother would be dead, stalked and shot to death by Joel, her then ex-husband from whom she had managed—for one glorious year—to escape. In the weeks following her death, I turned to poetry—the only language that seemed capable of containing my immeasurable grief, as in these lines from Lisel Mueller's lovely poem "When I Am Asked," about why she began, in the aftermath of her mother's death, writing poetry: *I . . . placed my grief / in the mouth of language, / the only thing that would grieve with me.*

A few weeks after my mother's death I wrote a single poem, and then I stopped writing. Perhaps I carried the guilt that somehow my early desire to write for the pleasure of it—because I loved the stories I was reading? because within the pages of a book I could escape to other worlds, leave behind the psychological abuse and constant threat of my stepfather?—I had somehow created the situation in which she'd risk his violent retribution to protect that desire, to nurture it. Thinking I had been protecting her, I had remained silent about the many ways he tormented me.

In the moment I stopped writing, I had also shuttered the articulation of my grief. It would be several years before the absolute need to articulate the depths of that trauma, the facts of it and the way it connected in my psyche to the legacy of White Supremacy—its ongoing manifestations—would lead me back to poetry, making it such that I had to write lest the twin pulls of my existential wounds destroy me.

———

When I wrote the notes for a draft of "Permanence" in my journal, opposite the page on which I'd written the words "natural disaster," my mother had been in the ground only five years, and although I had finally begun trying to write elegies for her, I saw no connection — even though the *unnatural* disaster of her death haunted me. In the years that followed, I became increasingly interested in the national trauma of civil war — a kind of domestic violence — and the further psychic violence of our national amnesia around the role of black soldiers, the marginalization of so much African American history, buried and forgotten.

I had by then reached the point in my life at which I had lived as many years with my mother as I had without her. I had spent the years since her death trying to erase as much of the memory of those difficult years with my former stepfather as I could, and, in the process of my willed forgetting, I had begun to lose her as well. Without writing the story of our lives, her tragic death, I was grieving in silence, reinhabiting the violent silence of that household in Atlanta—a victim of my experience, not the master of it. To have dominion over oneself, to be the sovereign of the nation of the self, one must be the writer of the story. That I have come to be a writer in the aftermath of my mother's death still wounds me: she nurtured the very thing that could engender my survival in that house, despite what it meant for hers.

Not until I was at work on what would become my third collection of poems, *Native Guard,* did I finally see that my obsessions, my existential wounds—the bedrock of why I write—were inextricably linked, and had been all along. *Our metaphors,* wrote the poet Mark Doty, *go on ahead of us.*

The realization began with an examination of buried history, pulling me again back to my childhood in Mississippi. Every year on the Fourth of July my grandmother would take me for a picnic on Ship Island. It was part of a string of barrier islands just off the coast of my hometown, and the site of Fort Massachusetts, which had been occupied by the Union Army during the Civil War. Although we were guided through the fort by the park ranger each time we visited, there was a history we never learned during the tour: that black Union troops had been stationed there.

The first regiments of the Louisiana Native Guards had been mustered into service in 1862, after President Lincoln issued his preliminary Emancipation Proclamation: the first regiment becoming the first officially sanctioned black soldiers in the Union Army, and the second regiment assigned the duty of manning the fort on Ship Island as a prison for Confederate soldiers, military convicts, and prisoners of war. Even though it is a national park maintained by the federal government, a plaque placed at the entrance by the United Daughters of the Confederacy inscribes only the names of the Confederate men once interred there, and an obelisk in the center of the fort memorializes their treasonous cause. Nowhere on the island is a similar plaque or monument memorializing the names of the Native Guards who served and died there — and if tourists didn't know to ask about the history of these black Union soldiers, the park ranger most often overlooked this aspect of the fort's history in his tour, mentioning only that this was a fort taken over by Union forces and that Confederate prisoners were kept there, leaving out an important American story about soldiers who had been slaves before enlisting and their valiant role in preserving the Union — a whitewashed version of the island's history.

Encountering Civil War history in school — even in literature classes — I could see that black Americans were written out of the story or presented only in the backdrop as slaves. "The real war," Walt Whitman wrote, "will not get into the books." Studying Whitman's *Leaves of Grass,* despite his open-armed enthusiasm, his inclusiveness and celebration of everyone, even the lowliest prostitute or degraded slave — a poetics of democracy — one could still measure a significant absence. In high school, when my teacher discussed the poem "Reconciliation," we learned a narrative of "North and South, brother versus brother," that did not include black soldiers, even as Whitman had encountered them in the military hospital and had written about seeing the Louisiana Native Guards on parade in New Orleans. The poem presents a metaphor for washing away the terrible events of the war and the way nature is complicit in that washing, that erasure.

RECONCILIATION

Word over all, beautiful as the sky!
Beautiful that war, and all its deeds of carnage, must in time be utterly lost;

That the hands of the sisters Death and Night incessantly

    Softly wash again, and ever again, this soil'd world;

. . . For my enemy is dead, a man divine as myself is dead;

I look where he lies white-faced and still in the coffin — I draw near;

Bend down and touch lightly with my lips the white face in the coffin.

Here, Whitman suggests the reunion of the nation, men on opposite sides of the war drawn together beneath the banner of reconciliation. However, in the final image of the dead — a repetition — "white-faced" in the coffin, Whitman leaves out the reality of so many dead soldiers whose faces were not white. And further, according to the historian David Blight, the poem highlights — in the "kinship" of the dead white brothers — "the ultimate betrayal of the dark-faced folk whom the dead had shared in liberating." Not to mention the black dead who had also fought for that liberation. Though Whitman had acknowledged black soldiers in his letters and reminiscences, ultimately he often left blacks out of his larger concerns: "When the South is spoken of," he wrote, contrasting the roles of the ruling class and the masses, "no one means the people, the mass of freemen." Here, Whitman is referring to the free white masses, even as his language presents an opening that reminds us of the invisible *freedmen* all around the South. In fact, according to Daniel Aaron in *The Unwritten War,* "the Negro did not figure significantly in [Whitman's] calculations for America's future, the Grand Plan of History."

That the historical erasure of black people in the larger landscape of American cultural memory is a given, a distortion of our shared history, was for me an invitation to write into the absences in the record — an act of redress. "Poetry," wrote Percy Bysshe Shelley, "is the mirror that makes beautiful that which is distorted." Researching the lesser-known history of Ship Island, the black soldiers to whom no monument there had been erected, I had found an entrance, a path to follow, a metaphor. I began work on the Native Guards intending only to reinscribe their history into our collective cultural memory, but the act of writing held the mirror up not only to my nation but also to myself. It hit me one afternoon when I had been running in the cemetery near my house.

There was an old section there, full of the graves of former Confederate soldiers. Perhaps because I had been writing poems about black Union soldiers, something compelled me that day to read aloud the headstones of each of the Confederate dead, and I stood there quietly whispering their names into the wind. Back home, I sat at my desk as if to answer some call, thinking I'd write a poem about them. What came out instead was a poem about the day we buried my mother, "Graveyard Blues," a poem that takes the classical form of a sonnet and marries it to the vernacular form of the blues.

GRAVEYARD BLUES

It rained the whole time we were laying her down;
Rained from church to grave when we put her down.
The suck of mud at our feet was a hollow sound.

When the preacher called out I held up my hand;
When he called for a witness I raised my hand —
Death stops the body's work, the Soul's a journeyman.

The sun came out when I turned to walk away,
Glared down on me as I turned and walked away —
My back to my mother, leaving her where she lay.

The road going home was pocked with holes,
That home-going road's always full of holes;
Though we slow down, time's wheel still rolls.

I wander now among names of the dead:

My mother's name, stone pillow for my head.

When I finished a draft of the poem, I pondered the last couplet: the idea — implicit in the lines — that, missing my mother, I could go to the cemetery and lay my head against her name on the stone: a communion that would be cold comfort at best, but a comfort nonetheless. It was one of the emotional truths of the poem, but in terms of the facts it was a lie. And in that moment, I knew it. And I knew the real question I had been asking those many years ago when I began trying to write "Permanence": *What will keep her from being erased, forgotten?*

What did it mean that I was both the one who was forgetting her and the one whose native duty as daughter was to remember? I had turned my attention to public history, to national trauma — the domestic violence of civil war — instead of contending with the hidden truth at the heart of what I had been writing. To confront my own complicity in erasure and forgetting, to tell the truth, I had to write another poem, "Monument," that answered my lie in "Graveyard Blues."

MONUMENT

Today the ants are busy
    beside my front steps, weaving
in and out of the hill they're building.
    I watch them emerge and —

like everything I've forgotten — disappear
    into the subterranean — a world
made by displacement. In the cemetery
    last June, I circled, lost —

weeds and grass grown up all around —
    the landscape blurred and waving.
At my mother's grave, ants streamed in
    and out like arteries, a tiny hill rising

above her untended plot. Bit by bit,
    red dirt piled up, spread
like a rash on the grass; I watched a long time
    the ants' determined work,

how they brought up soil
    of which she will be part,

and piled it before me. Believe me when I say
I've tried not to begrudge them

their industry, this reminder of what
I haven't done. Even now,
the mound is a blister on my heart,
a red and humming swarm.

The metaphor in the poem's final stanza reveals the truth that hit me that day I went running in the graveyard: *what I hadn't done.* It suggests the ways that I had not properly tended to her memory, her gravesite where the ants are building a monument—another word for ant mound—that I had not yet built. In all the years since her death I had never put a headstone on her grave. She lay in the ground unmarked, not properly memorialized by the one whose *native* duty it was to remember. Like those black soldiers, she had been erased from the monumental landscape. My metaphor had gone on ahead of me; finally, I had begun to catch up with it.

The collection came together, then, at the intersection of personal and public history, erasure and memorialization, and vernacular and classical traditions.

Traditional forms serve as not only a container for grief but also – as with the repetition of the blues – a way to transform it as well as a means by which to reinscribe narratives that have been erased: the necessity not only to say something, but to say it *again*. Thus, I made the most use of received forms rooted in repetition and refrain: the crown of sonnets, the villanelle, pantoum, ghazal, palindrome. These forms, too, are monumental.

Audre Lorde wrote: "the master's tools cannot dismantle the master's house." I know of course that she was referring to the myriad tools of oppression from laws to custom all rooted in the thinking – powerfully metaphorical – that shape our perception of others, the social reality we create in which to live. But when I read her words, I can't help but think of the received forms of poetry I learned in school – sonnets for example – and how I have turned to such forms to contain the subject matter necessary to challenge the master narrative. In that way, I believe the traditional forms – the masters' tools – can help in the dismantling of a monolithic narrative based on racial hierarchy, willed amnesia, and selective remembering.

Nowhere is that narrative more oppressive than at the literal monolith to the Confederacy in Stone Mountain, Georgia. Carved into granite—the largest bas-relief monument in the world—are the enormous figures of Robert E. Lee, Stonewall Jackson, and Jefferson Davis. It loomed over us the last year of my mother's life, when we had escaped my former stepfather. We lived in an apartment near its base, and my mother died in the shadow of it. To realign the world, I write to create a monument in words to her—a palimpsest overwriting the inscription of White Supremacy that loomed above her death as if to render her life, our lives, small and insignificant.

Writing *Native Guard* revealed to me what had been forming all along: the absences wrought by historical erasure were an opening into a field of thought, the native pastures in which my intellect and way of seeing had been cultivated—not as limitation but as something infinitely generative. As in a photograph in which someone has been cut out—the empty space, a hole letting the light shine through—the absence becomes as palpable as the former presence.

There would still be revelations to come, but at that point I understood something about metaphor and pattern and palimpsest that I had first begun to learn on long walks with my father along the median of a highway that was once a pasture, picking wild-flowers for my mother and listening to poetry; in my grandmother's workroom, hearing again the sounds of her humming above the rhythm of her foot tapping the pedal of the Singer sewing machine; in my mother's voice as she sang to me, overwriting the inscription of the Confederate flag with the possibility of justice.

The first elegy I was able to write for my mother, nearly fifteen years after her death, transports me to the backyard of that house of my early childhood. It's called "Limen," which is the physical threshold of a door but also the threshold to an emotional or psychological state.

LIMEN

All day I've listened to the industry
of a single woodpecker, worrying the catalpa tree
just outside my window. Hard at his task,

his body is a hinge, a door knocker
to the cluttered house of memory in which
I can almost see my mother's face.

She is there, again, beyond the tree,
its slender pods and heart-shaped leaves,
hanging wet sheets on the line — each one

a thin white screen between us. So insistent
is this woodpecker, I'm sure he must be
looking for something else — not simply

the beetles and grubs inside, but some other gift
the tree might hold. All day he's been at work,
tireless, making the green hearts flutter.

The poem began as a memory of standing in the threshold at the back of the house — just as I had stood when the whole yard was a field of water — and seeing only the faint impression of my mother like a pentimento behind a swath of the white, blank erasure of a sheet: the invitation of paper before the words appear on it. It was as if I were being given an image of what was to come: the barrier between our worlds, thin as the line between life and death. But in the act of writing, I found that she could be resurrected for a moment, rising to the surface of the page, brought back in the imagination through the sacred language of poetry, the bittersweet pleasures of elegy. I have turned to literature for the way it enables us to momentarily suspend time, to live in the moment of a story unfolding, or within the lyric articulation of the self, wherein the intimate voice of a poem, the rhythms of thought, reanimate in the mind — both for the writer and the reader. In that act of reanimation, the language of poetry creates a space for what I've lost to carry on, a momentary stay against the inevitable.

What surprises me in trying to articulate now why I write is that there is something I can see that I had not allowed myself to acknowledge before, even in writing my memoir. The longest chapter of the book is the first one, in which I spend a great deal of time describing my early life with my parents at my grandmother's house in Mississippi. It took me years to write it because I did not want to leave that time and place. To leave it meant leaving my native geography, the security I felt in that house at the crossroads, for Atlanta. It also meant remembering the things I had spent most of my adult life trying to forget. It took me seven years to write the book, and, in that time, I began to have a reoccurring dream that always takes place in my grandmother's house, always in the current moment.

The dream begins in daylight, in my feeling of contentment at being back home, even though I am in the house alone. As night comes on, whatever relief I initially felt being back in that place of security, of unconditional love and happiness, goes away. Up and down the hallway, I walk from room to room, checking the windows which, I see now, will not fasten. In the kitchen at the back of the house, the deadbolt will not engage, and I cannot get the door to fully close. Everything has only the appearance of being locked. Though I can't see anyone or anything outside, I am struck with the awareness that only my own vigilance will keep the house secure from whatever awaits.

Each time I awake from this dream I am deeply troubled by the way it turns to nightmare: that the feeling of being so vulnerable, so unsafe from external forces, occurs inside the house of my happy early childhood, the place of refuge and respite in which I was able to dwell for three glorious months every year. Despite everything that has happened, the dream never takes place in Atlanta.

But of course, the language of dreams is not literal. Only when I think of my grandmother's house as a figurative place can I see what the dream has been telling me: that there are always existential threats; living with grief and survivor's guilt, and in the aftermath of trauma—both personal and national—the potential for what might lie in wait, ready to reemerge, is imminent. Writing is a way of creating order out of chaos, of taking charge of one's own story, being the sovereign of the self by pushing back against received knowledge and guarding the sanctity of the dwelling place of the imagination, that place of first permission.

I return often to the shotgun house at the crossroads of Jefferson and 49, the highway that was once a pasture. Although the house no longer stands, its contours are etched deep in my psyche, and I find myself opening again and again the doors to its perfect rooms, the myriad chambers of memory: one room leading into the next, the very architecture of thought.